The Beautiful Borderline

For Janie Fannon, who was kind.
For Laura, Emma, and Patti, my trinity of roses.
For Hanna, Arthur, Rachel, and Darren.
For my BFFS Dave and Alex G.
With love to everyone
always.

The Makeshift Child

The Makeshift Child

Mother and young child
separated at the department store.
People come to help.
For an eternity, among the unfamiliar faces I cry.
When my mother is finally found, she is
happily shopping among the hanging clothes.

In the hands of strangers you must learn
to love yourself.

Bedroom doorknob releases in my hand.
The door locked, I spend hours screaming,
panicked.
I could open this window,
climb out onto the roof,
past the starlings, past the pigeons roosting,
but I will not keep going.
I could step out onto the clouds and
walk happily up a cobblestone path to heaven,
but I will not keep going.
I will come back until she notices me.

Behind all locked doors you must learn
to love yourself.

Pisces Rising

On the second story of a red brick house
a gray door opens onto a small balcony.
Reaching into evening, a few
things are left out,
a plastic tea set upon a
wooden table, a doll,
a child, a stuffed green dog,
a small black train going
round and round on its tracks.

The child has thin blonde hair,
the kind her grandma says would go up in flames
if she stood too close to a fire.
She sits among her toys singing quietly to them,
pretending as the door closes.
Birds come only so close but
cats can climb branches and ledges
and sometimes cats can be perfectly positioned
at tea tables, for a few seconds.

Her songs are small. Her heart is a sponge.
It is a quiet thing, a mind imprinting
on the breeze.
Tiny raindrops mist her hair as she hums a
song about cats and birds and all things small.
Beyond stolid black trees
a thousand gray doors open in the sky.
Behind watery blue clouds
a full moon rises.

Whisper

In the morning I wake with you,
a child robbed of innocence.
Having found you where they left you,
I hold your hand.

We pretend to hear the wind through the cat tails,
a humming through the trees.
I tell you, nothing is true
but the sound of your voice.

I am a child myself.
Someday you and I will grow into dark willows,
then into the purple sky
beyond these weeping branches.

We will live
no longer for angels,
or devils, or prophets,
no longer for show.

How far away our journey will take us
to the last star, and then back, to begin again,
to fingers returning white dolls to their shelves,
fingers returning touch softly.

How sad the child who must pretend,
who has felt the ugliness
of hatred through
his skin.

You are the blind child I will carry,
the tiny one I will love.
I tell you nothing is true but
our hands and creation.

For I can smell the roses flowing
through the red streams in your hair,
and I can taste the ocean air
inside your blue palm.

I have heard your voice calling
always,
the sound of truth hidden,
yet still felt deep inside,

a child's truth,
covered in all things kept,
buried in all things felt,
cloaked in that whisper.

Childhood

Falling down,
letting others pick you up.

Head stuck between banister poles.
Tongue stuck to a frozen, metal gate.

Legs up against a shiny brass bedpost,
wondering how they'll change.

Big teeth.
Big laugh.

Holding pinkies as you balance
on a fence.

The city is an ocean. It tides go
in and out.

People warm you
quietly from a distance.

People leave the wrong way and then,
the darkness of a dreamworld settles.

Stuck, beautiful weed,
you grow tall,

past all kinds of
love.

The Stray

The cat has come today, a street cat.
Small and gray, it polishes itself before me.
I open the packet my mother
was kind enough to buy.
The smell from the bag fills the space
between Cat and me.
She comes a little closer.

I am talking, not noticing her hunger,
talking as a bag opener, a mother,
and a friend, until she wonders aloud at
the length of time I am taking
and I stop to ponder the furry person
standing in front of me,
large eyes and skinny legs.

I feel sorrow at her need, and
at the hunger that causes her to
meow in the company of both
soft and harsh people.
It is early summer. My mother is
asleep. My father is gone.
My grandmother is far away.

The apartment complex is a cold gray.
I have found a friend named Sylvia,
an older lady who lives down the block.
Each day is the same.
I wait patiently as Sylvia opens bags
of goodies she has made
especially for me.

The Puppy

The children across the court have found
a puppy, accosting him with all the
affection given a pinata.
They hug him, poke him, squeeze, and chase him.
In the grass he makes his way to me,
small, brown, soft, panting in my lap.
I touch him softly, bending my arms and
body around him to protect him from the children.
I'm unaware that it will not be long
before I have a puppy of my own that I am
loving because I've been loved, that I
am hitting because I've been hit.
This puppy, he looks at me in a way I have
not been looked at before and he rests, does not
want to leave me when the children come
to dance away with him.
Before he goes, he takes one long look at me
maybe asking why we are so tired.

Orphan

The path still in sight
will fade through the night
and tomorrow it must be ignored.
There is no peace of mind
in the dreams left behind
and today is its only reward.

As the leaves glide along
they are whispering a song
of a child left alone for so long.
Here's a soft, quiet tear,
one for each passing year,
and two, for each minute you're gone.

Who Am I?

Who am I
hardening into stone?
What strength will I know?

That I am not a leaf
which caused itself to grow.

I am one hand pressed into
the stars, and one into
the snow.

Awkward Growth

Tonight a little girl sleeps in
a bed made just for her,
in a room she knows as hers.
Her lungs open and close themselves harshly.
Her chest heaves and fights the cool air.
The woman who sleeps in the room below is there
readying the car, waking the man who will
drive them to the hospital. She is phoning
her sister-in-law next door who is a nurse.
The woman is always there,
scurrying about like a worried squirrel.
It could have been that she thought the
little girl would stop growing this night.
But it was that the girl let her worry,
let her fear, so the girl would not have
to do these things,
so the girl could live.

She is standing at the edge of the
hospital bed, looking relieved and
happy for the child's care.
The room is bright white and the grandmother
is smiling. All can see how much the
child is loved. No one can see how strange
the child feels inside at love's receipt.
No one can know that this night is not
about sickness or pain, but
awkward growth.

Little Ghost

In these moments
I am standing at the top of the stairs
wishing to be more than human.

These chemicals, this body,
are a dream I can
wake into for some short time.

Even so young, I know, I would choose
nothing more than to stand here,
listening to the music of her voice.

I am small, as small as that moment in
which the earth learns it is growing
and so dying.

I am a sudden creation,
standing at the top of the stairs,
breathing myself in.

With labored breath and little lungs
that fight the cool air,
I stay quiet as she sings…

and wait in the shadows of my childhood
to become a little ghost,
floating down into her arms.

Sing to Trees

If someone calls you ugly,
smile into every mirror you see.
If someone says you are hopeless,
look up at the hopeless stars.
If someone says you don't matter,
feed a starving child.

If no one will listen as you speak,
find yourself a rhythm and sing.
If someone tells you to be quiet,
sing to trees.
If someone succeeds in silencing you,
paint them a lullaby.

Free

I'm eight years old. My mother
is ill, drawing

pencil sketches of houses, over and over, which
she will build someday.

She blends into the couch - orange and
brown like burning leaves,

dryly scoffing at the news and at me,
coffee cup in one hand, cigarette in the other.

I am sitting here silently alone inside the
poison mouth of my mother, my home.

Night after night I sleep on a lice-ridden couch
afraid of death and this gray town,

its businessmen, bartenders, and broken veterans,
the people who pass through me at school,

its empty alleys and tired travelers inside them,
the old abandoned five and dime building,

the yellow clock eye of the courthouse dome
blinking bats into the night sky.

Bent set on never growing,
I am growing.

I am enamored with the winter-white U.S. landscape,

the way the earth smells in spring,

bright twinkling stars on a warm summer night,
and the beautiful colors of autumn.

Each morning I walk out into the world
smaller, all the while learning the

flirtation and the winsome smile,
the please, and the thank you,

the shoveling after winter ends,
and what everyone should do, but can't

to carry you out, and
let you go.

Eyes

Everything is quiet.
The house is a chaotic stillness.

The plumbing broken,
I wait for the rubber band to break.

I wait for someone to come, but
they don't come. They never do,

not my smiling grandma at the door
or even a stranger.

So she takes me there herself, to an
agency that helps kids,

and I meet a man with eyes going in
different directions.

He talks to me about my life,
my filthy house, my mother.

I do my best to listen to him
while I'm trying to follow an eye.

Though I have a big family somewhere,
grandparents, aunts gossiping like

cackling hens, quiet uncles
and cousins who don't live like this,

I will be going to foster care now.
But it might not be so bad.

People will look in on me,
maybe the skinny nervous lady

or the chameleon-eyed man,
or a new person.

Maybe I will be one of the lucky ones,
around people who touch me softly,

or who look at me with soft
eyes.

Someone Must Have Said

Somewhere,
somehow, along the way,
someone must have said

this is not your fault,
none of this is your fault
dear child,

but I must have been watching
the TV too loud,
or playing with my dog,

listening to the radio,
Toto's *Africa* was on
and I couldn't hear their

whispers above the music.
Gonna take a hundred
men or more…

Walk Away

On these walls are white mushrooms, brown
mushrooms, gauche green and orange flowers
bowing to each other,
dancing to the hum of a transistor radio.

I'm six months old, sitting in a sea of olive green.
The shag carpet tickles my skin.
An ironing board stands between me and the bedroom
door. I'm reaching for something.

You walk away, cigarette in hand.
The silver iron grows hotter and
smoke billows beneath it, turning
a white blouse to gray.

A small flame multiplies, spreading across the
now-trembling board.
The fire steps swiftly,
orange teardrops and ashes drip to the floor.

Its path is clear, to the blankets and the bed, the closet
near the door you left through.
Minutes pass. A wall of heat
rises in front of me and I, happily unaware,

look up to see you standing in the doorway,
paused, as if deciding our fate.
In your mind, then, and everyday thereafter,
you turn to walk away.

Foster Care

They are a couple who have offered to share their home.
He stays up with me for a late
night snack of ice cream
wondering about my life, wondering what is in my
head…wondering.

At the next place, children surround the foster mom's
body like little mice, scurrying around happily for her
attention.
Big woman. Big chest.
She hugs you from a mile away.

Another couple, this time reserved,
cookies on the counter uneaten confuse me.
Big religion, the Anti-Christ, the Rapture, things I do
not understand.
I do not understand

other people's homes, open, yet walled off.
Laminated. Opaque. Secretless.
Though I wait with them, I cannot touch their
dustless shelves.
Don't they know, I'm not this doll.

Belonging

The orphan speaks of parents,
of sitting on a park bench at dusk between
the two steady, soft walls of them,

of bats flying over a small lake toward the three,
tiny sharp-edged black bats
turning into butterflies.

The two parents are castles, and the child, a little
moat they cross back and forth into
their own belonging.

The Nuns

They tell us to relax.
Relax in bed, sprawled out.
Don't sleep in a ball.
Are they relaxed in their stiff
habits in church?
Sister Clara has whiskers.
She shakes a little girl who decides to
stand on a toilet seat in the restroom.
She chastises a little boy for
kissing the cheek of a
girl out on the playground as
the church bells sing.

In the halls I have tape on my
mouth. In class, though I've
memorized the rosary, I
won't compete with the others.
Instead, I'll draw a picture of a man who
loves Christ leaning against a rock.
While I draw, the world goes away.
I almost don't notice Sister Clara
bringing Mary Ann to the front
of the class for talking and
the ruler coming down hard upon
her frail, white hand.

The Alien

Somehow I remember mothers and storms and
asthma and bees.

I remember being hit and my father taking
pictures under the orange sun,

my cheeks flush from running and my eyes bright.

I remember being poured into guest glasses and
praying for rain.

I remember the cool, black soil of the
earth and the winding,
blowing branches of trees.

I remember my grandma working on her knees in
the white kitchen,
my grandma dreaming of white stairs.

I know I came upon so many realizations late.

I know the thing that gathers itself up to flutter against
my ribs is a small, red silk thing,
a beautiful thing.

We came upon the sky in flashes.
I can still see our lights like a slow-motion storm inside.

I was wondering what I was then,
but there is no need.

Paper Dolls

Your head is close to
mine again.
The shape of your face
aligns my neck.
My eyelids are closed,
a wall of trees
circling around me.

Shall I wonder at you
always from the inside,
or come out to dance in the wind,
for the feel of the air,
for your laughter,
your touch,
for a place to begin.

One Hope

As a child I'd sit upon a short stone wall
studying blades of grass, fingering weeds

with small thoughts of my
relatives' hopeless love,

thinking of my grandmother
and all the human weeds of her garden

stabbing each other for her
light and kindness,

how she and I had chosen
each other, our dependency,

both of us waiting
for something we couldn't name.

Now I realize, she had named it
Him and I had named Him peace,

our one hope gently
placed into separate boxes.

A rosary became a leaf-filled branch,
the bible opened to a bright blue sky,

the floor of a tall church filled with warm
sand and holy water, our healing tide.

The School

Why do adults on trains never smile?
Love is on a different train, rolling past them through the
night.

When I am 13, my mother chooses a boarding school in
the northeast to leave me, 500 miles from my
grandmother. After, she slips into the cracks of Arizona's
deserts, a hermit crab
set free from a glass jar.

The train taking me back and forth to the school from
my grandmother's town rushes and stops,
rushes and stops. I sleep for a while, feeling sick from
the movement. Then, leave my seat to be
part of the movement.

I travel through the cars like each is an adventure,
wondering to myself why adults on
trains never smile. The cars are wild silver bullets,
connected by thin, metal slabs, shifting,
bumpy and precarious under my feet.

In the dining car, a tall, skinny man sits behind a bar, his
brown face and lips
drawn downward like a frog's. The shiny black hair
surrounding his
neck curls up like a female's.

The eerie dark lighting of the car enhances his smiling
features as he asks me if I want anything.

He is the frogman from
Alice in Wonderland and there is a
strange music playing in the car.

Thirteen hours later,
the train stops in a dirty city where there is a layover for
the better part of a day.
Here are a few small glimpses of a
bustling gray freedom.

I sit for a while in the train station,
sketchbook in my hand, drawing a bearded man from a
distance. Another man,
drunk and smelling of urine, is escorted out of
the station by security.

Outside, the city is gray and dusty. I go to eat at a nearby
restaurant and leave a
big tip for the smiling waitress.
Down the street there is an adult bookstore.
I've come here before.

This time, as before, I stand sheepishly waiting to be
noticed by the cashier.
In this store filled with adult books and videos,
somewhere in the back are
personal movies you can watch for a quarter.

I ask the cashier almost every time I come if I can see
what is back there.
Again he tells me that I must be eighteen. He is a fat,
black man, a fat Buddha sitting
surrounded by his adult mysteries.

I talk to him, this time for a long while.
He says when he was about my age, he got a perfect
score on the SAT's. He speaks intelligently and
I believe him, as if he is
a polished statue among filth.

The city is made up of swirls of color
behind the dirty doors.
In its center is a large mall with every kind of store one
can imagine. I spend hours
walking, taking it all in.

At the top of a tall escalator I trip,
catching my balance and losing my sunglasses.
I watch them fall, gliding easily
down the long stairs,
breathe a sigh of relief and move on.

Though nothing is mine, I'm still happy.
In everything I find possibility.
I live in these few hours the life I will come
to long for as an adult,
belonging only to myself, carrying nothing.

At 5pm a bus comes close to the station to
take me the 45 minutes back to the
boarding school. Inside its rectangular buildings
 I will be forgotten and
then I will forget myself.

Years will pass, a few vacations, more glimpses into
freedom will come.
Each of us travel to the school in our own way.
It is a long journey, no matter if the bus

or train ride lasts minutes or hours.

Some of us will become lost somewhere out there
between the school and *home*.
Over the years I've come to realize,
maybe it is only the very strong
who do not return to either.

Easier to Believe

The girls in the school, I'm not sure if they're scared.
Some of them are bullies. I know some of them were
beaten and hurt by their parents.
I know some of them were loved by
parents who are now dead. Perhaps a few were
untouched altogether, the quiet ones.

I think the house is too clean. The furniture and walls are
straight-lined mazes in the bland 70's style.
Beige carpet stretches on forever, empty and forlorn.
I play my Phil Collins' cassettes all the time.
He sing to me in a voice full of passion, anger,
confusion, and tenderness.

The other girls like Boy George, Madonna, Michael
Jackson, and Wham. But someday I'm going to London
to meet Phil. I'm different from them.
My prom dress doesn't even look like theirs. A male
teacher was paid by the school to take me to buy it,
pink puffy sleeves and tiny white dots.

There is a rumor that a girl here is pregnant. Her room
smells of vomit and she will be leaving soon.
What happens to her when no one was there to begin
with? What happens to the child of the child?
She'll find out, or maybe she knows already, this glass
house is not the world.

I haven't heard from my mother in years. I see my
grandma two or three times a year but my father says I
cannot visit her this summer unless I lose weight.
Despite all this, I usually do not cry like
some of the other girls.
I think maybe it's because I am nothing.

Dreaming of Love at Sixteen

If I had a love, he would be my shoulder,
the part of my back I cannot touch
and so am not quite sure about,
but soft, and still a part of me.
We would have a house,
each night another night in the
dark of our rooms,
our bed of flowers, our tasseled windows
full of stars, the hat box with its
stray cat resting quietly,
the picture of my grandma, the mirror,
the masks and the children.
Each night the same smile,
the same candle lit.

If I had a love
he would be my clouds and my anchor.
I would grow within him
sometimes a quiet storm, sometimes a rose.
And I would come to him as he is
sleeping, gather him up into my
childhood dreams.
We would walk the ocean's floor,
share our stories with the snail queen
and the giant clam, this strange deep love.
Then when morning comes we would hold
each other's hand and take our first
steps out into the concrete that lies
beyond us,
stronger, one because of the other.

Rooms

For Ken

On the outside I'm pale white and have long
black hair, but inside, you can walk into my
psyche like it is a room.
It's up to you whether you feel comfortable.
The black furniture is soft. You can't really see or feel a
window because the room itself is the sky,
dark blue, purple, and black, and the stars are filtered,
bright white without accosting you.

Sometimes I pretend there's a wall here
separating me from God.
Sometimes I hang up the face of an angel, a jester, or a
child on this wall.

To know yourself as a room, always the same room,
is a stable thing. Even though it really shouldn't matter
what anyone else thinks,sometimes it does.
For a while, they were treating me as if I were white
with all white furniture. In the middle of this all white
desk in this empty white room, there was
a green dot, just sitting there, looking like a pill.

Other times, people think I'm a rainbow of the colors of
Easter, maybe a room that collects statues of the Virgin
Mary or small elephants or salt and pepper shakers or
children. It takes time to know who you are and even
more time to be okay with it or to change it,
so every once in a while it feels really nice when
someone lays their head back and tells me that it's really
comfortable here.

There's always that place inside you, you know, a place
that no one sees unless you let them.
You can always know who you are that way.
I have a friend who started creating his room really
young. He needed to.
He'd been beaten and raped so many times.
He needed control, everything to be in its place.
He needed peace.

There is soft music flowing in his room,
and art, and stars like mine,
and when I go there I can fall into his gentleness so
completely, sometimes I never want to leave.

The Dorm

我爱你

The dorm's halls are white and
hard and cold.
Inside the rooms there are girls
with nothing and everything in common.

My roommate is straight A's.
Her mother calls her every day.
I make fun of her, but I am not
smart enough to know why.

In the study room, the girls talk about oral sex.
One girl says it's gross.
I don't say anything because I know I will
share everything someday.

There is a quiet girl that I follow.
When she was young,
her father dyed her hair to
have a blonde child.

One night, my roommate and I
lie in the dark, counting
the virgins,
counting the fast girls.

Some of them sit in the hallway, listening.
Finally, one gets up to shout at us through the
vent in the door, scratching
her crotch feverishly.

The girls ask me to dinner.
I say no and eat by myself.
Soon, there isn't enough space and
A Chinese student comes to join me.

He is far away from home.
I ask him how to write something in Chinese
and he blushes.
我爱你

Innocence

I never knew someone could only want the outside.

Secrets, lies, my universe grows smaller.
One decision has a ripple effect.

We were young and foolish but, trust,
you've taken what was left.

Nights like these are portals,
doors we cannot walk through without changing.

Just a kiss, an airy whisper blowing the weight of
my soul into yours.

Pass it back to me refined.
Rest your heated palm along my ribs.

This moment…the ticking of a small, white alarm clock.
The rhythmic drip of a bathtub faucet,

planets rising and falling, apathetic, oblivious to the
sound of jeans unzipping.

Can I have my innocence back? *My pride.*
And in the morning become the eager child I was.

In the daylight can I run somewhere,
anywhere, to bury my regret in

the garden with the gray dog,
or at the muddy foot of a tall pine tree,

in the warm, dry sand beside a palm,
or at the base of a small, white church

where shiny leaves the color of blood
fall silently, one by one on

the frozen November ground.

Believe

The arms that hurt you are not your own.
The words that destroyed you were never yours to speak.

You are free to choose a different path from their pain.
You can choose who you will become.

Planted in the shade, you are whole, beautiful.
Standing tall alone, you grow through darkness.

Someday you'll grow high enough to see light
through the dark clouds and swaying branches.

Until then, do not give your life away.
Your desires are real; they have worth.

Do not give your dreams away. Acknowledge them;
pursue them unless they hurt another.

Alone in your own skin, though not in spirit,
someday you'll find others who understand.

There, in the brush by a crystal blue lake, behind
tall weeds and cattails, you'll find the other swans.

The Makeshift Woman

Apple and Worm

And he enters her
biting into her innocence

closed upon her,
his tongue moving over the white,

rocking slowly,
the two together,

fruit and fruit's conquestor,
heavy and light,

red fruit falling into
baby's palm.

Young Woman With A Paintbrush

(explicit)

From the endless expanse of space which appears black
to us, a white body, stick-figured in shape emerges.
Uncertain, it turns back toward the black as if
questioning a fall, a push, or a decision.
The next step moves this body into a world of color and
heat. It walks, taking in the earth's vibrations.

It meets a man. The man sees the figure as small and thin
so he judges it to be a woman.
He takes her by the arm quickly, into a series of rooms.
Just as quickly, he throws a soft pink blanket over her
head and body. She must have hair, long
and brown. She must have a face.

Her eyes will be green, the man says,
with long dark lashes.
She will have full lips and breasts.
When he is done, she has all the parts of a woman.
He says he will show her trees now and blue oceans and
stars that fall out of sight beyond the horizon.

Then he rapes her. When he is done, she has all the parts
of a baby growing inside her.
When the man is sleeping she runs far away to find a
room in which to hide. The pink blanket will not
come off. It is holding the baby. Nothing will come off,
not the eyes, nor the hair, nor the lips.

When the baby is born, the woman picks up a paintbrush
and paints the whole of the baby white.
She breaks off its hands and feet and cuts off the hair and
dangling skin. She paints over the eyes and the nose.
She sits, holding the infant as it dies, painting on canvas
after canvas, a faceless figure running toward silence.

Whose Heart Will Stop Today?

We play God, never asking to play.
We ask to be set free.

Driving in silence to the women's clinic,
clouds and the sky merge into one milk-blue sheet
falling down on everything,
faded blue like the clinic walls,
no red, no pink.

The girls in the waiting room look healthy,
not poor. They look cared for,
holding leather purses,
in jeans or slacks, with neatly combed hair
and pensive faces.

They read magazines, looking up as quickly as
they look back down, waiting for
their ultrasounds and consults,
peripherally absorbed in the quiet
movements of the office.

They sit together but alone in a
small circle, looking like children who
are too tired to stop a game of
musical chairs, ring around the rosy,
or duck, duck, goose.

The Makeshift Woman

First love, I'm all in and
you begin to pull away. I don't have
those sea-foam blue eyes to crawl into
and rest any more, this sanctuary.
I'm scared and alone.
I don't know us and
I don't know the world.
In the hands of strangers you must learn
to love yourself.

In the unwed mothers home,
most of the young girls will keep
their babies. The one who doesn't, who
goes through with the adoption, has
a mother who visits her every day, smiling,
no pressure, just support.
I try to call you, but you do not
accept the calls. You send me a letter, an
apology and a goodbye.

I could open this window,
climb out onto the roof,
past the starlings, past the pigeons roosting,
but I will not keep going.
I could step out onto the clouds and
walk happily up a cobblestone path to heaven,
but I will not keep going.
I will come back until he notices me.

Behind all locked doors you must learn
to love yourself.

Your Cry

Alice in Wonderland, my favorite book, my life,
every person was crazy, each insane in their own way.
I had no choice but to believe what they taught me,
that everything was my fault, the child's fault.

I couldn't touch. I couldn't love, until a young man came
along and I loved him with the passion of ten
borderlines, which sent him floating away like a helium
balloon, higher and farther.

And now, I have you here, and I should not have a baby.
I should not have you with me, young, penniless, and
alone, but I cannot let you go. *I cannot let
go of the little girls we are.*

They wished it and now I am gone from the world and
myself. *Though somewhere deep inside I still believe
love is enough, I know nothing but the fear of being
alone. I hear nothing but your cry.*

God Was Gone

I did not follow His rules.
I made the real world up in my head,
kept a baby bird in a styrofoam cup
instead of a nest.

We lived wounded under a bush,
away from the security of a tall tree.
I did not think of Him,
because He did not think of me.

She and I, we met the world together,
its changing fears and joys.
We trembled at animals eating animals,
at boys killing boys.

We dreamt of love, of sunsets,
of nights with full moons and laughter,
but all we could see were branches
holding up a waning moon.

And the cats crept at night,
when I would stay up listening,
my body, a barricade of flesh.
I never slept.

Adoption

I am a flesh house aching for calm every day.
I am a house my daughter runs in every day, upstairs,
downstairs.
In the ghetto, we cannot always walk
out of the door of me.

Virgo sun, Gemini moon, Pisces rising,
I've locked myself into a dark place, a dragonfly beating
its head
against a cellar window. The clicks have become a slow
song, drummed by distant thunder.

We can't get out of each other here,
this symbiosis.
In these crossed worlds, pleasures suffocate us, our lives
bought on credit, possibilities eclipsed by
my selfishness.

I sometimes carry us out to a new place for a day.
We drive by nice houses in towns next to lakes, next to
churches,
houses filled with contentment and peace,
happiness.

I give her up to these houses in my mind,
to a childless couple waiting with open arms,
families, weddings, vacations, and picnics,
summers at Grandma's house, holidays full of color and
promise.

I love her.

Stubborn

The buses take us back and forth
through different shades of gray
into more questions.

And when we have no money to
ride them, we walk back from the
welfare office, me, twenty years old,

you , two months old, sleeping in
a carrier on my stomach.
The twenty-five blocks to the apartment, we walk alone.

On the way, two businessmen walk past us,
their low pockets jingling heavily with coins
as the buses roll by.

Four Round Dots

The pen that I am writing with is
fluorescent green.

She's laying next to the page I am
attacking with my thoughts.

Watching the bright pen move
back and forth, she wriggles,

learning to handle
her infant legs and arms.

Sometimes if she looks at me from a
distance, her eyes look like perfect round dots.

Her face is as round as the sun and
just as radiant.

She's pudgy, no muscular, and
what a smile. It covers half the sun.

I have created a healthy wonder,
a special little girl.

Innocent, waiting,
what does she want?

What does she hope for?
Perfection?

Or just two round dots looking back
at her, smiling…

Baby

You are two years old.
The purple storms that pound us
have just begun. I find
I try to hold onto moments
like they are tangible,
pink weapons to brace myself with
against the future,
as if the memory of innocence
will sparkle lavender and light
through all sorts of hurts.

We travel on different buses
here and there inside the
city doing errands,
today, rained upon at every corner.
You've gotten used to being pushed
everywhere inside your thick, blue stroller.
It is September and a chill
is in the air. Yellow leaves are wilting
atop the cement.
We are both tired,
returning home just before
the dark settles outside.
I pull you from the stroller into my
arms and hug you.
You open your little fist and I see the
crackers you've held in your
hand for hours are
warm and dry.

Hanna's Moon

I had you too young, when I was too young to fear you.
I had you alone, though I rarely knew otherwise.
At two, you loved to smell roses and tulips.
You wore strange hats and walked on velvet,
bumping into fire hydrants because you were
always looking up and everything you drew in the sky
was real and beautiful.

There were ponies and unicorns, three-headed dragons,
fairies and cherubs, two suns and a silent moon.
I thought maybe it was a dream and
I would wake up, that you
were here and I had so little to give.
I never knew silence was deep gray-blue eyes and tiny
soft hands learning to hide things.

This cruel, beautiful world I could not explain,
but it took no money to carry you out beneath the night
sky when the moon was full. I remember I would say
"Hanna, the moon, look how bright, look how warm",
and I thought you'd stolen it.
I remember I would say "Hanna, the moon, look how
bright, look how warm", and you looked.

OCD

I am not moving, but quaking inside as I stand on
a city sidewalk at noon.

In a daycare yard which seems so far away,
I have a daughter imagining cloud shapes into ponies,

the same clouds which on this day dropped a
baby bird at my feet.

On its side, it watched itself die, shaking,
and I in mourning stood startled as businessmen

and women walked past us quivering messes,
no dead creatures anywhere.

I stood watching for movement,
wanting to pick it up and cry like a child.

Hugging it with sorrow only, I took on its fear,
its humility and its death movements,

without meaning to, took them home and
practiced, to make the memory perfect.

Alien Love

I take a huge pot out into the backyard.
We make soup, everything expired or yucky
like oatmeal we dump into the pot.

Neighborhood kids come and
begin adding things from the ground.
After, they run races around the yard then

come in for a drink of Koolaid.
They've wondered about the new girl and
her child living here among them.

When it is time to go, some of them
linger outside by the window and
stand watching our family of two,

their small faces looking into our warmth.
How long will they wait tonight
in the window, witnessing my daughter's hugs?

A loud voice calls some of them home
to doors that have been
locked since morning.
.
The rest wait a while, then
walk away with their heads down,
tiny silhouettes fading into the dusk.

Home

What are we witnessing?
We drive quickly past these places, these faces.

Outside in the ghetto the sun's rays glitter down
filling a puddle by a bus stop.
A little girl gets on bus number 8, following strangers.
Her mom has locked the door and her older brother,

five years old, has found a funny pipe along
the sidewalk. If they bring the little girl back it
won't matter, no one to listen to
her voice behind the doors.

We are tough young ladies who seem to have to
fight to live. I've made so many mistakes
I can't count the sunsets I've missed.
I stayed where they put me because they put me here.
My unheard words are my life. They speak about
everything, the gunshots, rats, cockroaches,
the violent fights,
the music, the screams, the breaking glass,
here, where police don't dare to drive at night.

Morning rays of the sun hum over each personal
wreckage,
and in the afternoon, the rolling by of buses,
kids squealing down the back alleys toward ice cream
trucks,
one child less than the day before,

pigeons as big as chickens searching the dumpsters,
gang members searching for fathers and brothers,
milestones celebrated in quicksand,
desensitization to sirens and the cement life.

Makes no sense to live this way and to keep
living this way but if we try to relearn,
to break ourselves in half teaching our souls that
we are worth something, take a chance on leaving,
do we really ever find our way home?

Ghetto Child

Foreign smells,
fights,
actors without agents,
broken streetlights,

shouting,
guns, spring's gray sky,
the last plant to die,

no clock,
no calendar,
no cereal and toast,
just bones and blood,
gangs,
a frightened mother
holding bodies close,

morning tears and
crack-pipes, a
new mouth to feed,
rapes,
burns,
thundering music,
fear,
needles,
broken glass,
condoms,
roaches,
birthday candles,
sweet sixteen.

Someone Else's Tomatoes

For Shonda

Can't afford a depression.
Can't afford to stop losing myself.
With all my babies can't afford a subway ride out.

One, two, three, Sade sings about me.

Home to her three kids after
her gig, daddy's out makin' the fourth with
someone else.
Got a neighbor to watch them.
They have my nerves to erase every day
and my bones to hang themselves from, play on.

I'm healthy. I'm young. I'm beautiful.
I brought these children here into
this makeshift world,
a party in the ghetto.
I didn't know there were other places,
other people to be.

Sometimes we take a walk together past
a nice yard and look at
each other, sad,
over someone else's tomatoes.

I save up my money to buy toys and books
and I teach and teach and teach.
Sometimes I look into the mirror and I see myself
somewhere in there,

*and I look back in time at my grandma who held me
tight and I whisper "I'm sorry".*

*And I go on, month to month, forgetting myself,
washing away, tending, bleeding,
holding a little hand.
June,
September,
December comes.*

*The dry burnt air of the furnace
pours out and the familiar
smell reminds me
of all the Christmases I've built.*

America, Going On

A utility center in the heart of poverty,
daily payments preventing disconnections,

We are human cubes inside an ice box,
sitting, waiting for our names.

One glass door says use the other door.
The two o's of door have been made into

angry red eyes. A large woman, newly styled hair
sits above the crowd behind a large, white desk.

Sheet of paper taped in front of her, behind her,
beneath her say CONTROL YOUR CHILDREN.

A little girl comes in with her mother, smiling,
resting her arm along a soft blue dividing rope.

The mother's hand comes down twice upon the child's
arm. The little girl still knows how to cry.

Next door there is a carryout where the
lottery is played and food stamps are accepted.

Beyond the store, there are apartments, doors
without screens and windows without life.

Few things interrupt or ease the long, hot

minutes of August. The air on the steps is

conditioned with speculation, need…
momentary howls at the children.

Barefoot babies use sticks to mix dust in the holes of
a sidewalk. Diapers dance close to the street.

One woman follows the mail cart to her neighbors. All
guess on behalf of the mailman, she will have her check

in twenty minutes…Five minutes pass…Ten…the
afternoon will never end.

Fifteen. A bucket of water comes out toward the
dusty children.

Shrieks. The golden envelopes appear
and something in the air has lifted.

Women on porches and in kitchens breathe some small
sigh of relief. Something in their mothers' faces

start the children laughing. Women and men set out
toward the sound of buses, of cigarettes being lit

and of America going on, dividing itself.

The Depression

I know she's out there somewhere. I know the world is
out there. I just don't know where or how far
or what to do in the daytime.

The office is another tired city building,
a gray empty space with artificial light,

poor ventilation, dusty books, a forgotten aquarium
with a small goldfish, diseased, and raw.

I am looking at the outlines of all things,
not at the center, as I take the stairs shakily, heavily.

Speaking to no one, I try to connect with my
fingers on the railing, but they are not mine.

I tell the psychiatrist that I am detached, that I
wish someone could punch me so I could feel.

I tell her that nothing is real, that everything is different,
a gray fog everywhere, suffocating me.

She asks me if I see things. *No, it is what I don't see.*
She asks me if I hear things. *I say no, but*

there is a jester laughing in the distance.
She says I can function out there if I take it slow

then swims back into the comfort of her books as
I leave the building with clouds in my neck.

Beyond the gray horizon a wild, white sun burns my
eyes. Sideways toward home I move tired and numb.

The pollution of man spreads into my body again.
Moving awkwardly, I take strange breaths in my hurry to

be slow. I feel movement around me. I see white waves,
a hollow vibration, a window full of light opening above.

I close my eyes and call her name softly.
My swollen belly floats up to meet the sun.

Trapped

My wheelchair pulls
me away from freedom,
happiness, dances,
first kisses.

I am angry, fruitful,
angry, nurturing,
angry.

And all that I have been given
is time to count the drops
of frustration
underneath the refrigerator.

How does one end what has
not begun?
On a cold January morning
I scream chalk along the boards
and smash the white walls pink
because he didn't call
or called too softly
or called my bluff
living this ghost
to its fullest.

Gray sunshine, dead birds,
dizzy fly in my bathroom,
smashing a different eye each
second, into the illusion
of choice.

The Lovers

As much as they can touch,
they touch,
gray needles threading
each other,
water treading water.

Here lies a wish,
here, a spine trembling inside
half of something real,
touching,
beginning to feel.

The lovers, someday as
much as they can part,
they will part.
How easily then
one will undo the other,

like dark roots torn from
the earth, all at once
nurtured, all at once free…
all at once saying goodbye,
not believing goodbye could be.

Dreams

I saw a little boy on a tricycle
and the smiling boy's form fit the bike's
form so completely,
it looked to be one complete figure,
one yellow, red, and blue baby animal
steering through the afternoon shadows,
oblivious to my dream.

I saw a warm house made of gray stone
with an arched white door in its center.
The sidewalk, flanked by bushes and
flowers and two marble lions,
sent itself out to me
but never stopped, so I could see the
couple who lived there.

Karma

Karma is no one's
friend or enemy,
but an aggregate of stars,
with arrows pointed
ever
forward.

It awaits you in your next life,
an impassioned lover,
a frightened child,
a mother at peace
with her baby's
healthy cry.

It is the eternal turner of pages,
a chess master awaiting
your next move.
It is old love and old hate
meeting new skin,
yet knowing.

Karma,
neither friend nor enemy,
is the voyeur of
unrealized dreams,
and the accountant of
little bones.

Belle Luce

For Hanna

As we stood next to each other, gazing
through that big Victorian window at the
twinkling stars and crescent moon,
crisp white sequence against dark blue felt

I wish I would have known
that the universe would take care of us,
that there was no reason to fear
and no cause to question things.

Our lights, *all our lights*, are here to brighten this
world with art, peace, and compassion, this beauty,
and you, little one, were on your way to
becoming the brightest beacon.

Social Worker

They wonder how I know
why the child kicks, cries, doesn't cry,
or why the child thinks he is nothing,
talks of suicide, hates his parents,
why the little girl pulls her hair out or
runs away, why she doesn't protect
herself as a teen.

The black space inside, some understand more.
I visit the children in schools or
at home, and together unconsciously
we draw rainbows in the dark,
but the chalkboard psyche washes
off with each new hurt
and I visit them again.

I am a vessel of nourishment and understanding,
though I am also the same little girl I was,
struggling against a vacuum of chaos I
had no part in creating, just as they do.
Sometimes the words come easily.
This is not your fault.
You are beautiful within and without.

Tell Her

Tell her that this life is hers
to grow at will,

to plan and create
a garden, a company,

a group of friends,
a family,

a clean corner of the world
where all that she likes can be hers,

where all that she is
can belong.

The Love I Must Learn to Give

When I was young I ran to people,
ran into people, *crash*,
with no one to pick up
the pieces but me.

I'm beautiful, my heart is, I know,
but sometimes I'm as
twisted inside as a baobab,
unsettled as a tornado.

At these times, I cannot run to anyone,
because I know, no man,
no one, nothing can save me,
except the love I must learn to give myself.

Forgiveness

Conceived From Rape

Conceived from rape,
I found out when I was twenty-two.
A hush fell over the world for a day,
and then came a shift,
everyone still dancing to
music I couldn't hear while
I stood still.

Suddenly I knew
how different different was,
how some scars may never heal,
how Easters and Christmases,
laughter and meaning
fall away into days where
you are left proving life.

Sometimes it seems that
while others are playing against a
yellow sun on green grass,
hitting small balls into holes,
I'm pretending that this world
is not just spinning on, oblivious,
that it is somehow calling

for the weak to help the weaker,
for the bruised to tend to
the bruised, for the thirsty to draw
water for all, and for everyone to
listen to this new music,
so that both the wanted and
unwanted can dance.

Healing

My mother and I are usually able to talk now, though
then I was treated as if it was I who had raped her,
brought myself into being.

There is a part of us that is the same,
two children who are small and sweet,
and like summer and rain we are friends.

Together in those years, we knew we were scared,
that the world was dark, and all that had
been done to us was dark.

Apart from the drive-throughs, the window openings of
Dairy Queens, and the open doors of one or two
friends, we needed something.

Our life was an old red house corrupt with filth and
sadness, all manner of ghosts and
our mutual fight to belong.

Even with hindsight, I cannot guess her lessons.
I cannot live her pain.
I can only love her from a distance

and hope that somehow we forgive the world and
ourselves, and learn to do
what is best for both.

Crab Mother

How many different places have you traveled
trying to walk out of yourself.
Your bones would feel better in the desert.
Your head would be clearer in another city,
a small city, a big city,
somewhere far away from me.

How many silent years have I breathed you in,
no matter where you were drifting,
climbing to the heights of your elation,
sinking to the depths of your fear,
a small snail on your weak shell,
afraid to break free.

There is a song I came to know,
an unanswered question, a song with no end.
Where is the comfort and where are the arms.
Where is the space that is mine to be in.
Where is my mother,
my enemy, my friend.

Only one picture left in my mind of you,
frail crab walking sideways along the earth's wide circle,
yellowed and leathered by time and the sun,
trying to breathe the same air you breathed as a child,
carrying forgiveness now
instead of me.

Goodbye to my crab mother.
I have loved you here.
Find a soft, quiet place to rest,
to fall asleep, finally loosened from your shell.
With one strong wind your fears are gone,
and the sea is coming.

Blue Night

Forgiveness, Unasked For

Next to a river bordered by cement, I hold my face in my
hands, looking down.

Under the blue moon's glow I can make out your
Piscean fingerprints on the water's surface.

I've come here to forgive you at last. You never asked
for my forgiveness the way she did -

you needed to, though like a fish the words may as well
have been spoken into beer, little bronze

bubbles floating haplessly upward. Alcohol gave you the
soft cushion of not remembering how you hurt people.

Your voice is far away, your arms too, your big hands…
your purpose, I never figured out.

It was not my place to try.
It is now my place to come here alone, at peace on a

blue night, to wait for something at last, to flow
out of me and into you.

Traveling, Unraveling

His hip was twisted away from him in an accident,
twisted all the way from Ohio to Oklahoma.

He limped in constant pain, drank a lot,
intended to travel,

to go wherever one leg and a car would take him,
looked forward to it.

At the time of his death, he'd saved up 10,000 dollars
and his car was running fine,

with whatever he'd wanted to see still out there,
an old friend, waiting.

If she takes this bus to a new state, a new place,
she won't die, her body won't

fold in on itself, her heart won't gurgle
repeatedly, her bowels won't bleed,

her mind won't detonate itself inside
a four-walled room.

There are stimuli, walkways out of herself.
There are places to go, people to see.

There are trash cans to raid,
anything not to die.

I Think She is Dead

I think my mother is dead.
I haven't heard her voice in a while
and the earth feels lighter,
passionless,
no aching pressure across the rivers,
no cigarette cough across the states.
The air feels cool and moist.
I'm light and clean.
I think my mother is dead.

I think the shores have bid her goodbye,
and the trains never taken have shown her
their backs for the last time,
and the men never tasted whose small
brains she could eat alive with black coffee are
stumbling away from her empty room in a daze.
There is silence now, my white silence.
I think my mother is dead.

The phone may ring again and on the other
line, her small voice.
A postcard might arrive, or an envelope,
inside it, twenty dollars
in an unsigned card.

Ashes

My 16 year old got her driver's license today.
All day it threatened to rain, an empty storm
thundering in the distance.
At home, my mother's ashes arrive in a heavy box. My
husband puts them carefully in my bedroom closet while
my daughter changes into a new set of clothes
wondering where she will drive next.

There is a heavy black cloud in my bedroom. Like a
bruise in eternity, a bruise in time, these clouds which
thunder but never touch us are still absorbed.
The ice cream truck drives toward our house, music
blaring. My daughter is off like a shot, a three year old
again, braids flying, running toward something
familiar and exciting.
Ice cream trucks, rain clouds, and freedom.
She says it's the best day of her life.

Teenager

There is a placenta between us, filled
with things I do not understand,

fragrant dying wildflowers, blind unicorns,
wilting autumn leaves in brown-silver puddles,

storm clouds, wire-haired black foxes looming
over treetops, impulsivity,

rainstorms, hailstorms, snow,
Asian babies, stage actors, plays, and piercings,

boys and hormones, grades and money,
cars, friends, broken dreams and bright new dreams,

the violent red of anger and frustration,
the liquid transparency of fear,

somewhere far beyond the necessary madness,
a bright blue sky.

Lupus

The wolf has come to rest
in my doorway alone,
gone missing from her pack.

If the sun turns to shine upon her face,
she dawns a dark pink mask
to meet it.

Visitors come to the door -
she changes her shape to
welcome them in.

As she walks, something metal scrapes in the wind,
the rusty hinges of old shutters, dry bones,
a low raspy song filling the air.

I need my sisters; they are waves
comforting me. I need my sisters; they are
waves, carrying me.

We are lost from one another
in a dry forest. The sun bleeds through us
and the colors of clouds fill our eyes.

Aggressive men come carrying guns to
silence what they do not understand.
I need my sisters.

Once, we were young.
The days were long and fluid.
We ran through dandelions and cool grass.

Like every young flower
we ached to open up.
We ached.

Human

I have the whole world to worry about,
my daughter, my new son, my husband,
finances, health.
Not this.

Talking to me in the hallway,
I might as well be crouched against the wall.
But I hold my head up, trying to act as
if I have confidence.

Not this again.
This feeling that I am not good enough, *not enough.*
This knowledge that though I am in the same
space as you, I walked here from Jupiter.

My beginning and my path were different than
most everyone I knew, and I exaggerate the
differences further, magnify their importance,
until I have myself walled off again.

I know, we are all human. If you had my life,
walked in my shoes, you would too at times,
be crouched in the corner of your own mind
saying *not this.*

We feel pain and we bleed red.
We long to believe in something more.
We are both weak and strong
and love is an action verb.

I hold your hand when you are hurting.
I wipe your brow when you are sick.
I listen to the smallest voices, and all the things
that I have been through, created *this*.

The Quadriplegic Child

For Patti

I slipped her shirt
over her back,
above,
and saw the space inside
her twisted spine,

the dark line,
the beginning of a stream of
memories,
the beginning of a river of
unanswered wishes.

Over the bed I lift her
like a cloud,
a child on a tire swing,
a bird whose wings were broken
by the wind.

She explains how
someone should lift her arm,
the wrist first,
then her hands,
and mind the toes.

I go later that day with my
daughter to the skating rink
and notice all the children
circling the floor,
the rush of silver wheels and laughter.

Merauda

Next to a red brick school rests a
large, unclimbable oak tree.
In the schoolyard stands a
quaint little girl, smiling, who looks at life
in a different way.

In art class, the other eight year olds
draw straight-lined buildings with
rigid square windows.
Hers is the Parisian cafe she's never seen,
large windows, bat-winged chairs,
wine glasses hovering magically over
dainty round tables,
the building itself drawn in crooked, genius
angles by a gifted child who looks twice at
unclimbable trees.

Merauda, in 4D, lives in someone's
basement and does what she wants,
creates what she wants,
and breaks what she wants,
and is what someone, somewhere would want.

But life is a slow parade of strangers all with
similar displeased expressions
and all of them silent,
their eyes facing forward,
marching straight-lined in tandem,
then drifting away, as parades do.

Summer

Locusts hum against black walnut trees.
We rest together in a back porch swing.

Amid the fragrance of roses,
squirrels play, yellow wrens sing.

White halter tops and little bead purses.
Small country store across the street.

Warm July air moves through the house.
Crawfish surface in the creek.

Strawberries grow in patches out back.
Fish tank glows at night.

The moon rises behind a tall church steeple,
beautiful and bright.

Peace when she hums and hope when she talks.
Her rosary glows against the wall.

She looks down at the stable ground when she walks,
grateful for it all.

Yawning children in the pockets of her cotton dress,
fading with the setting sun,

a goodnight kiss, a dreamy sleep,
and tomorrow's summer song begun.

My Darling Dearest

An Easter lily,
you blossom still,
and I beside you wait,
to pick you up,
set you gently into Holy water.

You are almost less than an
apparition now. I carry you off
to the center of my mind,
the only one who
knew how to love me.

The afternoon's shadows
fill this clean white room,
me in a black smooth metal
chair watching you,
you, in the barns with the cows,

in the fields with bright yellow flowers,
in your father's arms.
You search the ceiling blankly and
say something soft.
I hear "Kelly, why does time matter?"

Instead, you have told me that
someone has stolen your shoes.
In this lifetime I have loved you,
mindless. You have loved
me, blind.

You have called me your darling,
your dearest, your Kelly girl.
I have been ugly here and you, so
beautiful and brilliant, found my
beauty and calmed my soul.

Inside the white-blurred shadows of
your memory, you smile and reach your
soft hand to me, whispering...
"You are an angel,
my *darest*."

Laura Rose

I will always think of beauty
as my grandma putting lotion on her hands
which were already softer than clouds.

I remember those hands, how they
took the stingers of bees from
the swollen skin of her grandchildren,
wiped tears, pared apples,
watered flowers in June,

held each baby like God would
hold His little angels.

All of us were dreams to her.

If I could talk to her now
I would tell her that it is autumn
and that the trees are
breaking against the white sky

and leaves the color of lifesavers
are lying on the ground,

that every time one of those leaves falls,
it seems,
a church bell rings,

and people from everywhere are walking
through this, laughing…

I would tell her that somehow,
time has stopped this way
and I can watch it all until I leave,
never knowing anything again

except that at one time I was small,
very small and running to her.

I Wonder Who She Would Have Been

She was both happy and afraid,
happiest when she talked about
God and her children.

Always afraid, I think maybe even when she
was laughing.

A different dress every day, she never wore pants,
except to wade into her basement which was
always flooding.
So afraid of water.

She sang high and proud in church,
and cried the day some town boys set it
ablaze playing with candles.

My grandma, all fear and pride,
gentleness and love,
were it not for all the children and the husband
who didn't notice his daughters,
the cooking and cleaning,
the sewing and mending, the endless chores,
what would she have asked of the
earth besides roses?

Who would she have become?
If her world had shown her that she,
this beautiful woman, mattered.

.

After he died, I remember noticing
my grandfather's large rosary
hanging limp against the wall.
Where before it had hung proudly,
its bright glow shocking me at night as a child,
now it looked small, pathetic, and lost,
my fear of him wilting with it.

The things we have internalized, we don't
unlearn easily, but we never unlearn love.
I believe she would have been a teacher.
She already was.

Greg

We spent hours together under a Virgo sun,
beneath and inside trees,

digging in the sand and dirt,
running through dandelions,

hiding from thunderstorms,
pretending,

so many summers, laughing, exploring,
swimming in the lake beside your house,

rocking on opposite sides of an inner tube,
invisible fish biting our toes.

Born on the same day, we were astrological twins
alive inside a deep, blue sphere, a sapphire coolness.

My childhood was blessed by you.
You taught me how to play and *be*.

I saw you grow into honor and kindness,
a good man.

My cousin, my brother, my eternal friend,
thank you for the mirror you held up to me.

Ghost Cat

In the dead of the night as you lie in your bed,
moonlight gliding through your window,
you are not alone.

Nor are you alone in the early morning as ghost cat shifts
her body against your pillow.
In between the dark and light, you must rest and heal.

History has brought us, lifetime after lifetime,
a resilience and propensity toward dreaming,
a love of furry things and music.

Outside, trees rustle rhythmically in the cool wind.
Night to day to night again,
a blue November sky drifts downward onto gentle grass.

Softly together,
under the same stars we sleep,
my paw on your chest, my breath on your cheek.

Silent Night

For Kate

Bundled up in my warm car, we sip our hot cocoa
and sing along to carols we learned as children,
Deck the Halls, Rockin' Around the Christmas Tree,
and Kate's favorite, Silent Night.

Soft white flakes dance against the windshield.
Wreathed lampposts shimmer, sending shadows of
haloed angels onto buildings.Curiosity guides us past
bright lights on houses and green trees in windows.

Kate's life is a slow moving picture,
a story of innocence, love, and the struggle to be heard,
a film with too many directors.
There are tolls to pay for dancing snowflakes and music.

She has just enough time to set her cup down in
its holder before she clutches her stomach in pain,
arching her neck over her shoulder,
eyes open, staring at nothing.

In a few moments the seizure passes, and she
is back once again, calm and bright.
She starts singing again along with the music,
then brings her thin, pale fingers up to sign the words.

Lost in the meaning and melody, she moves
her hands expertly, conducting an orchestra of
snowflakes in the car's front window.
In this moment, nothing exists but a baby in a manger

and the sweet song of one, tender and mild,
who has traveled a world only few travel,
bearing the most valuable gifts of all,
hope, love, and *heavenly* peace.

This February is Different

For Darren

Oak leaves sprouting a few tiny leaves
next to our apartment building,
little baby smiling, round-faced atop a
pile of snow.

More white coming... we go in search of
a new shovel at a hardware store.
We separate, walk down different aisles,
searching.

I see you three rows away, quiet,
thinking all to yourself, oblivious to my watching
and I realize how long it is that
I have waited for this comfort,

for someone I love to come in from the cold,
to take his shoes off and choose to
rest beside me,
to love me unconditionally, always.

This February is different
because love is all around me,
in laughter and hope, in the search for warmth,
together, looking forward instead of back.

Thank you for the simple things,
for being there to talk or just to hold my hand.
I cherish every moment with you,
my best friend.

Happily

For Arthur

I slide the door closed.
He opens it up.
He slides the door closed.
I open it up.

The lights are off
and the bedroom is black.
The closet he's crawled
into is black,

except for a smooth green orb
he holds in his hands,
a bright, plastic globe,
a gently held planet.

In its glow I see curves,
his smiling cheeks,
wherever the ball goes,
glimpses,

the corner of a book,
the sole of a shoe,
a soft green light along the
edges of all things.

I slide the door closed.
He opens it up.
He slides the door closed.
I open it up.

I slide the door closed.
He opens it up.
I am there,
happily.

Little Man

The sky is warm this spring day, his sky.
We must do a thousand little errands in this small town.

Little man, next to me,
two years old, doing things exactly as I do.

Spring in the year 2002 is no different than
it was a hundred years ago,

the same wet earth smell and life renewed,
plants that have slept through winter, brightening again.

He notices everything for the first time,
a bird's chirp, a chipmunk scurrying.

The whole world waits
for little man.

It's our time to teach him to be gentle and good to the
earth.
We stop to wonder at a caterpillar.

He picks it up carefully, knowing it is a life like his,
puts him down where he found him.

How long will it be before he knows what men
are capable of,

that there are men plotting to hurt us,
to pick us up where we crawl and throw us down hard.

He holds onto my hand as we walk home,
smiling with all the wonder of any bright child

inside a warm, beautiful world made just for him,
a fragrant green place where men are good,

where men are honest,
where men are not inherently evil or pious,

but where men who have been hurt as children,
are now aiming ignorance and hatred at little man.

Anger

Don't bring the war
outside yourself, or let
others wars in.

Learn to be calm.
Breathe in.
Breathe out, slower.

Imagine a white orb,
a forcefield of protection
surrounding you,

inside this,
nothing but
transforming peace.

No one can hurt you.
No one can touch
you.

All energy absorbed,
makes the orb brighter,
stronger.

Transform it
into something positive,
something useful.

Let it flow.
Let it heal everything it touches.
Practice this love.

Until

No one can be perfectly free till all are free
... no one can be perfectly happy till all are happy.

- *Herbert Spencer*

I am looking at you through these eyes
and this heart, through ever-changing lenses.

Until I know myself, I cannot know you.

I am reaching for something, somehow
always needing instead of offering.

Until I love myself, I cannot love you.

I am learning compassion and empathy for
every living being, including myself.

Until I forgive myself, I cannot forgive you.

Compassion for God

Forgiveness for God

We are bunnies in the backyard, startled.
The kids play too close to our nests.
When I hear their human voices chirping
the universe splits open
and pale storm clouds walk over my home,
silver blades edging closer.

I see you, big. You see me, small.
I see your white skin hurting us.
Narrower and narrower you see less and less,
in doing so, move away from our creator
though it whispers and shouts,
cries in pain and despair at your doorstep.

Some believe God is a mirrored image
in a clean window of a white house they protect.
I believe God is in every living thing,
a blade of grass,
a willow silently following a river,
an ocean, a star, the universe and beyond.

God is a beaten dog beginning each day with
forgiveness, the child who is a different color than you,
the schizophrenic streetwalker,
and the lonely neighbor next door.

God breathes eternal transformation inside each of us,
inside the ever-changing quiet chaos of our souls.

God, the subject of countless perspectives,
is a composite of all these images - yours, mine, ours.
It is only when we look through each other's eyes
believing each view is real and has value,
the puzzle completes itself
and we finally see.

The Beautiful Borderline

At Peace

After many years, am I still a lost child?
This time understanding my heart,

this time reaching out to the world, to friends,
at peace with who I am becoming.

My heart is a small beach full of life
and warmth.

You can come to me with sunlight or storms,
with light or heavy waves,

because now I know, all of me will not
wash away from your touch

In Solitude

We heal.

I sit listening to the chimes of birds,
to the wind moving through
branches and grass,
feeling the sun's
warmth on my skin,

watching a squirrel savoring a nut,
a honeybee resting inside a daffodil,
witnessing each creature's
perpetual task to connect,
to be useful.

I have felt alone
but was never alone.
Even the trees
listen and feel the music of my
breathing.

Misfits

All the days of our lives,
we feel our differences harshly,
searching for others who
look like us,
pieces missing,
hoping we match,

the dreamy adult,
the open book,
the friend.

Somehow we are all makeshift,
souls in transition,
beautiful, fallible,
vulnerable,
human,

trusting, hopeful, curious
children.

Be kind to yourselves.
Keep playing.
Keep believing love will come.

Compassion

It isn't my lesson alone
to love and do no harm to others,
to love and do no harm to myself,
to live in peace.

Mine was not the only childhood
formed upon a breaking wave,
nor the only heart who has
questioned its own beating.

I am not the only alien to have
wondered at my strange abilities,
or to have sung a song in perfect
tune that no one heard.

The body is tired, exhausted,
but the spirit is strengthening,
cautious yet ready for
change.

What has been learned by witnessing
pain, disease, unease,
is finally noticing,
we are less afraid together.

Love

If in the course of our
waiting, our disillusion,
and our thousandth little death,
a warm hand comes to gently touch us,
a kind face looks with
acceptance upon our own,

to see us as we've wanted to be seen,
to see all the world has stained in us as pure,
to sponge and sift and show us our new selves
with each word and each touch,
understanding our frailty and without
judgment, rendering strength.

If all this human honesty, this beauty,
for even one moment we
attempt to return,
we have loved.

Hold On, Sewly

Your thoughts were created by monsters,
handed down through generations…
negative, irrational beliefs,
cognitive distortions, self-hatred.

Chemicals follow suit.
They flood you with fear and dread.
I promise they will pass and they'll
change, if you let them.

It will take time, which you have.
It will take strength, which you have.
But if you leave now, you'll never know
the joy.

If you leave this world now,
you leave the child in you behind.
If you leave this world now,
you will never know the life that could be.

There are second mothers and third loves,
fourth chances, all the above.
In a world with so many,
there is more to life than emptiness.

So if in this moment, you find you
cannot love this life, please hold on,
white-knuckled, tenacious until
you can…you will.

And Sewly, if in this moment,
you find you cannot love yourself,
this I promise,
hold on, and keep holding on -

Someone Else Will Love You.

Reaching Through the Borderline

Never question the scars on your soul, the
tear-filled waves crashing hard on the rocks,
for a human thought is but a whimsical thing,
a wave in a deep sea of clocks.

The gentle sky weeps soothing rain -
the oceans breathe purpose for you
to touch and be touched, to rest and be healed,
alive inside deep sapphire blue.

Do not be afraid to go under
the cool waters of this great earth.
In the quiet you'll find that the stars have aligned
to aid your rebirth.

When you're ready, reach through the borderline,
the space between you and me.
From the dark depths of fear to the white light of peace
you'll break free. You'll break free.

You are free.

The Beautiful Borderline

My life was spent crying, hurting myself,
in fear of people leaving. They left.

Not knowing who I was,
disbelieving the mirrors strangers held up to me,

outcast and ugly because of this,
I hid inside armor forged in hate.

It took me many years to just *be*,
and many years to see we're all the same.

Alive for brief moments,
but beautiful for eternity,

we are all reaching toward each other through
the borderlines of our skin, learning to touch,

perhaps more important,
learning to love the depths inside.

Tethered for a short time to the earth
pulled down into dust storms,

praying for air and water,
we do leave each other, often to become stronger,

and in the next life stronger still
until there will be no more leaving.

My life was spent laughing, playing alone and with others, learning to love myself.

Tethered here for a short time, pulled up into mystery and praying for God's light,

we do leave the earth, but always with more love than we brought.

Soft

I live with the
shadows of angels
moving behind my ribs.

I see my grandmas' smiles,
the snapshot photos of their faces
as dusk moves in.

I walk with a blind man who
shares his music - locusts chirping,
birds singing through the seasons.

I touch the face of a child
whose need makes me humble,
who holds the hand of the child I was.

I walk the earth with strangers
who become my family,
and I thank them for making me soft.

Made in the USA
Middletown, DE
13 June 2024

55672476R00070